PRAISE FOR
POWER THOUGHTS

*"Louise truly was a revolutionary.
She left us with so many world-changing
teachings on self-love, loving others,
and acceptance. What an incredible
contribution she's made to my life and
the lives of countless others."*

Kris Carr, *New York Times* best-selling author
and wellness advocate

LOUISE HAY

POWER THOUGHTS

365 DAILY AFFIRMATIONS

HAY HOUSE

Carlsbad, California • New York City
London • Sydney • New Delhi

Published in the United Kingdom by:
Hay House UK Ltd, The Sixth Floor, Watson House,
54 Baker Street, London W1U 7BU
Tel: +44 (0)20 3927 7290; Fax: +44 (0)20 3927 7291; www.hayhouse.co.uk

Published in the United States of America by:
Hay House Inc., PO Box 5100, Carlsbad, CA 92018-5100
Tel: (1) 760 431 7695 or (800) 654 5126
Fax: (1) 760 431 6948 or (800) 650 5115; www.hayhouse.com

Published in Australia by:
Hay House Australia Ltd, 18/36 Ralph St, Alexandria NSW 2015
Tel: (61) 2 9669 4299; Fax: (61) 2 9669 4144; www.hayhouse.com.au

Published in India by:
Hay House Publishers India, Muskaan Complex, Plot No.3, B-2,
Vasant Kunj, New Delhi 110 070
Tel: (91) 11 4176 1620; Fax: (91) 11 4176 1630; www.hayhouse.co.in

Text © 2005 by Louise Hay • Revised Copyright © 2023 Hay House, Inc.
Cover design and Interior design: Lisa Vega • *Interior photos/illustrations:* Shutterstock

The moral rights of the author have been asserted.

The information given in this book should not be treated as a substitute for professional medical advice; always consult a medical practitioner. Any use of information in this book is at the reader's discretion and risk. Neither the author nor the publisher can be held responsible for any loss, claim or damage arising out of the use, or misuse, of the suggestions made, the failure to take medical advice or for any material on third-party websites.

A catalogue record for this book is available from the British Library.

Tradepaper ISBN: 978-1-83782-019-1
E-book ISBN: 978-1-4019-7410-7

MIX
Paper from
responsible sources
FSC® C013056
www.fsc.org

Dedicated to all of us
who want life to be easy.
Changing our lives for the better
does not have to be difficult work.
Thinking one or two new, powerful,
positive thoughts a day is the way.
One day at a time . . . and
life becomes sublime.

INTRODUCTION

This little book is filled with positive affirmations. Every thought you think and every word you speak is an affirmation. So why not choose to use only positive affirmations to create a new and fulfilling life? Day by day you'll find new ideas for how to make each day a delightful experience.

An affirmation is like planting a seed. You're always in the process of tending to your garden, and if you do so with care, you'll find that each day becomes more joyous than the one before it.

You have the power and authority to take control of your thoughts and your life. By reading these affirmations—one a day, several at a time, or just by opening the book at random—you're taking the first step toward building a more rewarding life.

I know you can do it!

— Louise Hay

1

I choose to feel
good about myself each day.
Every morning I remind myself
that I can make the choice
to feel good. This is a new
habit for me to cultivate.

2

I am always presented with
new and wonderful opportunities.
I flow with what is happening
in the moment.

3

I now accept and appreciate the abundant life the Universe offers me.

4

Love is the miracle cure.
Loving myself works miracles in my life.

5

Changes can begin in this moment.
I am willing to change.

6

I am pleased with all that I do.
I am good enough just as I am.

7

It is my
birthright to
live fully
and freely.

8

I allow my income to constantly expand,
and I always live in comfort and joy.

9

I recognize
my body as a
good friend.

10

I am the creative power
in my world.
I express myself creatively
as much as possible.

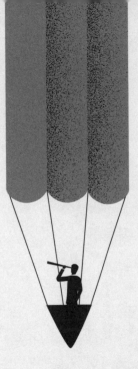

11

Good now flows into my life from expected
and unexpected channels.

12

My heart is open.
I am willing to release all
resistance.

13

I have the perfect living space. It is safe, and filled with loving thoughts.

14

I am one with the
power and wisdom of
the Universe. I have all
that I need.

15

I am unlimited in my own ability
to create the good in my life.

16

I breathe freely and fully.
Breath is the basis of life.

17

I have many dreams,
and I know that I deserve to have
these dreams come true.

18

My joyful thoughts create my joyful world.

19

I have my own set of talents and abilities.

20

I now release anger in positive ways.
I love and appreciate myself.

21

I keep my thoughts centered on
what I wish to experience.

22

I am equally blessed with love, harmony,
and joy. I take in life in perfect balance.

23

The Ocean of Life
is lavish with its
abundance. Golden
opportunities are
everywhere.

24

I see clearly.
I now create a life
I love to look at.

25

I allow my love to flow freely.
My supply of love is endless.

26

I feed my body nourishing foods
and beverages, and I exercise
in ways that are fun.

27

I love life! I am glad to be alive!

28

I am willing to
release the need
to be unworthy.
I am now becoming
all that I am
destined to be.

29

I feel good about everyone I meet. All my relationships are healthy and nourishing.

30

I forgive myself and set myself free.

31

I feel tolerance, compassion, and love
for all people, myself included.

32

It is safe for me to go
beyond my parents' limitations.
I am free to be me.

33

I only speak words that are loving, positive, and constructive.

34

I release all struggle now,
and I am at peace.

35

Life created me
to be fulfilled.
I now release all
expectations, and
I know that I am
taken care of.

36

No person, place, or thing has any power over me,
for I am the only thinker in my mind.

37

Every experience I have benefits
me. I am in the process of
positive change.

38

My body represents perfection.
I am vibrantly healthy.

39

I rise above all limitations.
I am Divinely guided and inspired.

40

I am mentally and
emotionally equipped to enjoy
a loving, prosperous life.
I am deeply fulfilled by all that I do.

41

I am joyous today. Humor and fun contribute to my total well-being.

42

Life brings me only good experiences.
I am open to new and wonderful changes.

43

I am always able to make
the correct decision.
I recognize my own intuitive ability.

44

My heart is opening wider and wider.
Love flows from me and to me in ever-
increasing amounts. I feel great. People
love being around me.

45

I rejoice in others' successes,
knowing that there is
plenty for us all.

46

Miracle follows miracle in my life.
I accept miraculous occurrences
in my life and in my world.

47

I release any limitations based on
old, negative thoughts. I joyfully
look forward to the future.

48

I always have wonderful, harmonious relationships. The person I am looking for is now looking for me.

49

Within myself I see
a loving, beautiful being.
It is safe for me to
look within.

50

My life continues to get better
and better. I now move into
my greater good.

51

I am the president of my own world,
and I act with honor and integrity in
all that I do.

52

We are all family, and the
planet is our home.

53

I focus on positive
thoughts because
the thoughts I think
and the words I
speak create my
experiences.

54

I am joyously exuberant and
in harmony with all of life.

55

I now choose to release
every negative, destructive,
fearful idea and thought from
my mind and my life.

56

I use my power wisely.
I am strong, and I am safe.
All is well.

57

Life supports me every step
of the way. I am fed, clothed, housed,
and loved in ways that are
deeply fulfilling to me.

58

I am worth loving.
There is love all around me.

59

I radiate health, happiness,
prosperity,
and peace of mind.

60

I move beyond old limitations
and now express myself freely
and creatively.

61

I trust my Higher Self.
I listen with love to my
inner voice.

62

I open myself to the wisdom within, knowing that there is only One Intelligence in this Universe.

63

When I listen to my inner self,
I find the answers I need.

64

It is healing to show my emotions.
It is safe for me to be vulnerable.

65

I open my consciousness to all the
wonderful possibilities of life.

66

I am safe in the world. I am comfortable with change and growth.

67

Whatever I need to know is revealed
to me at exactly the right time.

68

I see myself as a
magnificent being
who is wise
and beautiful. I love what I
see in me.

69

I recognize my body
as a wondrous machine,
and I feel privileged
to live in it.

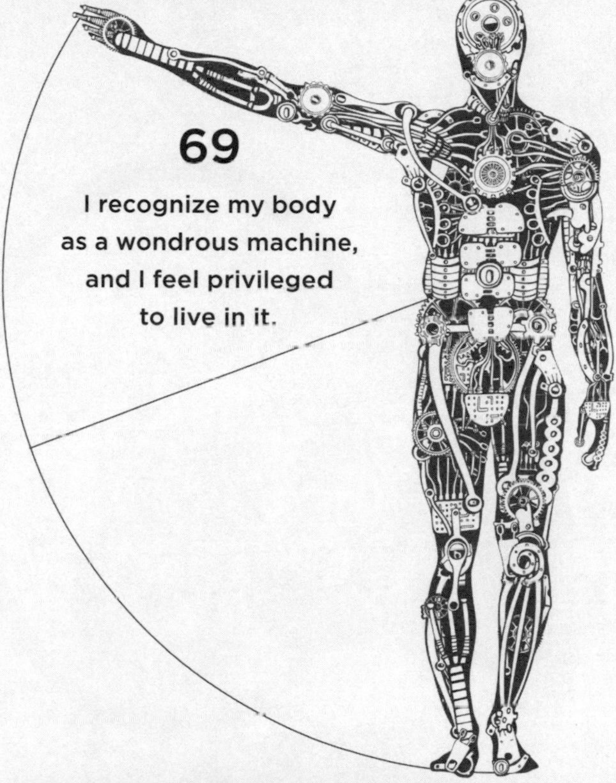

70

When I really love myself,
everything in my life works.

71

I am in charge.
I take my own power back.

72

I am good enough just as I am.
I approve of myself at all times.

73

I relax, and recognize
my self-worth.

74

I travel safely wherever I go.
I always meet loving, helpful
people on my journey.

75

I give myself the green light
to go ahead, and to joyously
embrace the new.

76

The people in my life are really mirrors of me.
My world is safe and friendly.

77

Today is my stepping-stone to new awareness and greater glory.

78

Freedom and change
are in the air. I discard
old ideas.

79

I am good enough.
Life is easy and joyful.

80

My body takes me everywhere,
easily and effortlessly.

81

I surround myself with
loving people who only
see the good in me.

82

I breathe life into my vision and
create the world I desire.

83

My life is joyously balanced
with work and play.

84

Divine Intelligence gives me all the ideas I can use.

85

I feel reborn. I am free from the past,
and I joyously welcome the new.

86

I see the best in everyone and help them
bring out their most joyous qualities.

I have compassion for my parents' childhoods.
I now know I chose them because they were perfect
for what I had to experience and understand.

88

I am created to succeed,
and I now give thanks
for my success.

89

The more I help others, the more
I prosper and grow. In my world,
everybody wins.

90

I am always on time, which is a way of showing respect to those in my life.

91

I speak up for myself.
I claim my power now.

92

I love myself exactly the way I am.

93

I am able to freely express my emotions at all times.

94

My body mirrors my state of mind.
I am healthy, whole, and complete.

95

I keep my thoughts positive.
Life brings me the good experiences
I deserve.

96

I am unlimited in my ability
to create good in my life.

97

I am lovable because I exist.

98

My uniquely creative talents and abilities flow through me and are expressed in deeply satisfying ways.

99

I am safe where I am.
I create my own security.

100

I am in the right place at the right time,
doing the right thing.

101

Every experience in my life is an opportunity for growth.

102

I allow the love from my heart to wash through me and cleanse and heal every part of my body and emotions.

103

I am grateful to others for the kindness they show me. I am filled with praise and gratitude.

104

I open my consciousness to the expansion of life.
There is plenty of space for me to grow and change.

105

Everything I touch is a success.
I draw prosperity of every
kind to me.

106

All my relationships are harmonious.
I see only harmony around me at all times.

107

Every decision I make is the right one for me.

108

I love who I am and what I do.

109

The past is over and cannot be changed.
This is the only moment I can experience.

110

I am at peace with the elements of nature.

There is no "good" or "bad" weather.

I can choose my individual reaction to it.

111

I stand in truth and live
and move in joy.

112

I create miracles in my wonderful world.
I am open to the wonders of the Universe.

113

I trust myself, and I trust Life
to support and protect me.

114

I earn an excellent income doing what satisfies me. I know I can be as successful as I make up my mind to be.

115

I am willing to
see how and
where I need
to change.

116

Today I do a mental housecleaning, making room for new, positive thoughts.

117

I am a Divine, magnificent expression of life.
Love surrounds and protects me.

118

I release the need to blame anyone,
including myself.

119

I am one with the very Power
that created me.

120

I give thanks for everything that
is lovingly supplied to me.

121

I now take care of my body,
my mind, and my emotions.
I feel good!

122

I constantly find new ways
of looking at my world.
I see beauty everywhere.

123

I bless and prosper others, and they,
in turn, bless and prosper me.

124

I envision a world of peace and plenty.
I feel harmony and unity between nations,
and I contribute to that harmony.

125

There is enough time and space
for everything I want to do.

126

Loving people fill my life, and I find myself easily expressing love to others.

127

I express gratitude to my own mother, and to all the mothers in the world who give their children love.

128

I love my family and my home.
I feel nurtured, warm, and safe.

129

I trust life to be wonderful. I see only good ahead of me.

130

I open my consciousness to the expansion of life.
There is plenty of space for me to grow and change.

131

I give to Life exactly what I want
Life to give to me.

132

I say, "Out!" to every negative thought
that comes into my mind.

133

I experience life as a joyous dance.

My body is ideal for me in this lifetime.

135

I release the pattern of procrastination within me.
I act with speed and resolve.

136

I look terrific and feel terrific.
Here I am, world—open and
receptive to all good!

137

I release any feelings of
competition or comparison.
I simply do my best and
enjoy being me.

138

All that I need to know
at any given moment is revealed to me.
My intuition is always on my side.

139

I ask for what I want.
I know that whatever I need
will always be there for me.

140

I trust in the Power that created me to protect me
at all times and under all circumstances.

141

I joyfully help wherever I can,
easing the load of others.

142

I rise above
all limitations.
I am Divinely
guided and
inspired.

143

I am special and wonderful.
The more I love myself,
the less stress I have.

144

I am patient, tolerant,
and diplomatic.

145

I expect my life to be good
and joyous, and it is.

146

I ask for more understanding so that I may knowingly and lovingly shape my world and my experiences.

147

I see abundance radiating all around me.
I now live in limitless love, light, and joy.

148

Every change in my life can lift me to a new level of understanding.

149

I create new memories
filled with peace, goodwill,
and compassion
for others.

150

When I find harmony
and balance in my mind,
I find it in my life.

151

I now choose to recognize the
magnificence of my being.

152

I respect others for
being different,
but not wrong.
We are all one.

153

I am led to fulfilling experiences.
I create a life filled with rewards.

154

I am very well organized.
Life is simple and easy.

155

It is always easy for me to
adapt and change.
I am flexible and flowing.

156

What I give out, I get back.
I give out only goodness and, in turn,
only goodness comes back to me.

157

I am willing to learn to love myself.

158

I break new ground
and begin exciting
new ventures.

159

I feel safe in the
rhythm and flow of
ever-changing life.

160

The past has no power over me.
I know that it is over, and I live
solely in the present.

161

I see my patterns and make changes
without embarrassment or guilt.

162

I cross all bridges with
joy and ease.

163

I experience love wherever I go.
Loving people fill my life, and
I find myself easily expressing
love to others.

164

I am at peace
with my sexuality.
I embrace myself
with love and
compassion.

165

I trust the process of life to
bring me my highest good.

166

I recognize that awareness is the first step in healing or changing. I become more aware with each passing day.

167

My thoughts are creative.
I constantly have new
insights and new ways of
looking at my world.

168

The answers within me come to my awareness with ease.

169

I respect my father for his love,
his good judgment,
and for just being who he is.

170

I know that the point of power is always
in the present moment.

171

I am willing to grow and change.
Every moment presents a wonderful new
opportunity to become more of who I am.

172

I am totally adequate at all times. I accept myself and create peace in my mind and heart.

173

No job is beneath me or above me.
If something needs doing, I do it.

174

I take full responsibility for every aspect of my life.

175

I love my body.
Every year I feel
more relaxed and
more attractive.

176

I deserve the best, and I accept it now. All my needs and desires are met before I even ask.

177

I express my creativity openly and freely.

178

I am willing to release
the pattern in me that is
creating any negative
condition in my life.

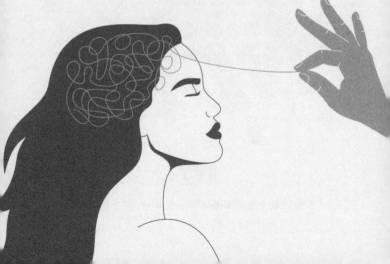

179

All that I desire, I receive.
I am fulfilled in all areas of my life.

180

I am my
best friend.
I love what
I see in me.

181

I allow change to occur without
resistance or fear. I am free.

182

I am perfect just as I am.

183

I give myself permission to be all that I can be,
and I deserve the very best in life.

184

I am totally free to choose thoughts of joy.
It is my Divine right to do so.

185

I embrace my entire being with
love and compassion.

186

I love who I am,
and reward myself with
thoughts of praise.

187

I release the need to blame anyone.
I accept the people around me as they are.

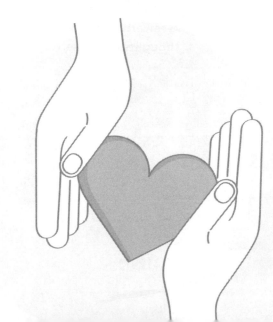

188

This is a new day. I am a new me.

189

Everything in my life happens in the
perfect space-time sequence.

190

Abundance is drawn to my every action.
I am a magnet for Divine prosperity.

191

I turn every experience into an opportunity.

192

It is safe for me to be flexible enough to see others' viewpoints.

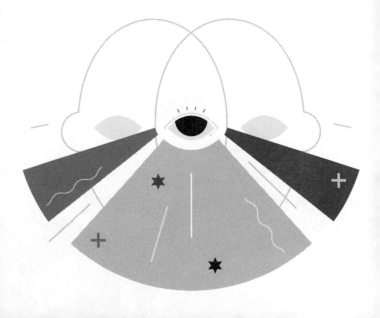

193

I have the Divine right
to be fulfilled in all areas of life.
I am worthy of success.

194

I easily flow with new experiences
and new opportunities.

195

I easily and comfortably release
that which I no longer need.

196

I am totally and completely supported by the Universe.

197

My body uses relaxation as a time to repair and rejuvenate itself. The more I relax, the healthier I am.

198

I speak up for myself
with ease.
I am intelligent
and powerful.

199

Every experience I have leads me to a greater
understanding of my purpose on Earth.

200

My income is constantly increasing.

201

Every problem has a solution.
Learning is easy and fun for me.

202

I am willing to grow up
and deal with my feelings.

203

Other people respect me
because I respect myself.

204

Only that which I no longer need leaves my life.
Everything that surrounds me serves a purpose.

205

I look forward with enthusiasm to the adventures of the day.

206

I expect life to be safe and joyous.
I attract all that is good.

207

My heart is open.
I speak with loving words.

208

I rejoice in what I have, and I know that fresh, new experiences are always ahead of me.

209

I have unlimited choices about what I can think.
My mind feels free and light.

210

I am now willing to
see my own beauty
and magnificence.

211

I am totally
adequate
for all
situations.

212

I now choose to support myself
in loving, joyous ways.

I listen with love to my body's messages.
My body is the picture of total health.

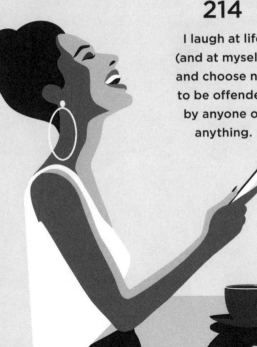

214

I laugh at life
(and at myself),
and choose not
to be offended
by anyone or
anything.

215

I handle all
my experiences
with wisdom,
love, and ease.

216

I am open and receptive to
new avenues of income.

217

I am enthusiastic about life.
I am filled with energy and optimism.

218

Every moment presents a
wonderful new opportunity to
become more of who I am.

219

I now choose to release all hurt
and resentment.

220

I see only harmony
around me at all times.
I am always safe
and secure.

221

I experience love wherever I go.

222

Compliments are gifts of prosperity.
I accept them graciously.

223

I am at home in my body.

224

I think positive thoughts, because every cell within my body responds to every thought I think and every word I speak.

225

I look within to find my treasures.

226

I am aware that what I do not want to change is
exactly what I need to change the most.

227

Whatever I am guided to do
will be a success.

228

Everyone changes, and I allow
change in everyone.

229

I accept myself,
and create peace
in my mind
and heart.

230

Today is a wonderful day.
I choose to make it so.

231

I accept perfect
health as my natural
state of being.

232

My understanding is clear,
and I am willing to change
with the times.

233

I take brisk walks in the sunshine to
invigorate my body and soul.

234

My body wants to be active and healthy.
Exercise is fun for me.

235

I am free to think wonderful thoughts.
I am in control of my own mind.

236

Love flows through
my very being.
It touches everyone
I meet and leads me to
greater compassion.

237

All that I seek is
already within me.

238

I forgive others, and I now create
my life in the way I want it to be.

239

I move beyond
limited human-mind
thinking and align
myself with the
infinite Divine Mind,
where all things
are possible.

240

I feel glorious, dynamic energy.
I am active and alive.

241

I rejoice in new growth.
I leave all reservations behind me.

242

It is my birthright to express myself creatively in ways that are deeply fulfilling to me. I have fun today!

243

I rejoice in what I have,
and I meet all challenges
with open arms.

244

I open new doors to life. New areas
of loving are always ahead of me.

245

I am in the perfect place at the perfect time.
I am always safe.

246

My life is a party to be experienced
and shared with everyone I know.

247

I work for enjoyment and satisfaction—
and not just to earn a living.
I use my mind and thoughts to enhance my life.

248

Life supports me.
It brings me only
positive experiences.

249

My inner quest is
rewarding and
provides me with
many answers.

250

I learn my lessons in life
easily and effortlessly.

251

Love operates in all of my relationships,
from the most casual to the most intimate.

252

My day begins and ends
with gratitude and joy.

253

This planet is my home.
I take loving care of the earth and
all the living creatures upon it.

254

I am always the perfect age
for where I am in my life.

255

I open my home and welcome guests with music and love. They are like a loving family to me.

256

I am willing to let go
of old beliefs that no
longer serve me.

257

My heart forgives and releases.
Inner peace is my goal.

258

Every experience
I have is perfect
for my growth.

259

I am organized and productive.
I am energetic and enjoy getting my life in order.

260

I release all criticism. I go beyond any feelings of not being capable and creative enough.

261

I am gentle and kind with myself as
I grow and change.

262

I use my Inner Wisdom to run
the business of my life.

263

The pathway to love is forgiveness.
I lovingly release the past and
turn my attention to this new day.

264

I expand my boundaries
to encompass only
positive experiences.

265

Knowing that friends and lovers were once strangers to me, I welcome new people into my life.

266

Life mirrors my every thought.
As I keep my thoughts positive,
life brings me only good experiences.

267

It gives me joy to take care of myself and others.

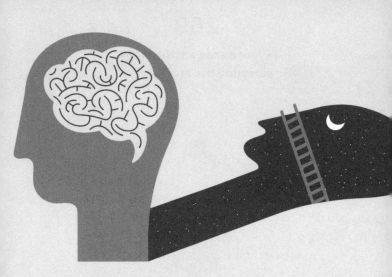

268

The Universe totally supports every thought
I choose to think and believe.

269

Divine peace and harmony
surround me at all times.

270

I release and let go.
I gladly give away all that
I no longer need.

271

My prosperous thoughts create
my prosperous world.

272

I rejoice in my body.
I am glowing health
personified.

273

I am independent, and I do what I want to do.
I try out new ideas. I am a leader today.

274

My life reflects good, and only good is reflected back at me. I am the cool, calm expression of life.

275

I always work with and for wonderful people.
I love my job.

276

My mind and body are in perfect balance.
I am a harmonious being.

277

I lovingly accept my decisions,
knowing that I am free to change.

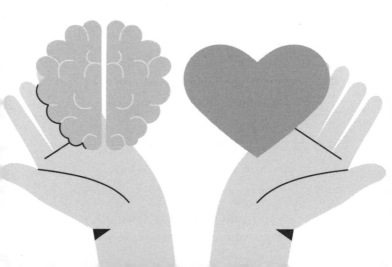

278

I constantly have new insights
and new ways of looking at the world.

279

I move forward with confidence and ease,
knowing that all is well in my future.

280

I become more lovable every day.
I am seen by others as a loving,
forgiving person.

281

I am responsible for all
of my experiences.

282

People respect me
and are very appreciative
of everything I do.

283

I radiate warmth and love.
I am beautiful, and everyone
loves me.

284

I awaken to my golden opportunities.

285

I now attract new friends who are exciting, loving, caring, accepting, funny, and generous.

286

I rely on Divine wisdom
and guidance to protect
me at all times.

287

I love life!
I look forward to every
moment of it.

288

Whenever I have a problem,
I know that it comes
from my limiting thought
patterns. I effortlessly solve
my problems by choosing
positive thoughts.

289

My home is a peaceful haven.
I put love in every corner, and my home lovingly
responds with warmth and comfort.

290

I express my emotions in joyous,
positive ways.

291

I am unlimited in my wealth.
All areas of my life are abundant and fulfilling.

292

I am grateful for life's generosity to me.
I am truly blessed.

293

I release all control to the Universe.
I am at peace with myself and with life.

294

I grow beyond my family's limitations and live for myself. It is my turn now.

295

I free myself and everyone in my life
from old past hurts.

296

Wellness is the natural state
of my body. I believe
in perfect health.

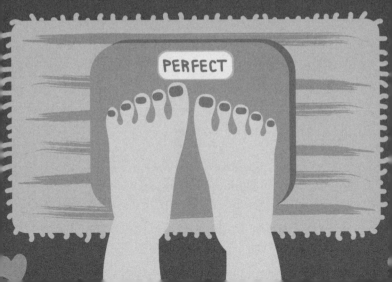

297

I am constantly moving forward
in the direction of my goals.

298

I am as successful as I make up my mind to be.

299

I respect and protect my body because
my health is important to me.

300

I open my heart and sing the joys of love.

301

Divine peace and love surround me and dwell in me. I trust the process of life.

302

I am in total harmony with my environment:
the sun, the moon, the wind, the rain, and the earth.

303

I dress beautifully every day because
doing so lifts my spirits.

304

I create peacefulness in my mind.
I trust my inner wisdom.

305

Every bridge I cross brings me to
a higher level of fulfillment.

306

I choose harmony and loving
communication wherever I am.

307

I appreciate all that I do.
I am the most important
person in my life.

308

Every person, place, and thing on this planet is interconnected with love. I am at home in the Universe.

309

We are all doing the best we can
with the understanding, knowledge,
and awareness we have.

310

I joyfully keep my inner child safe at the center of my being. I love and cherish my inner child.

311

Every moment
is a new beginning.
My life is so sweet.

♡ ♡ ♡

312

I am compassionate and understanding.
I forgive and forget.

313

With my loving attitude, I help to create a world where it is safe for us to love each other.

314

Peace begins with me.
The more peaceful I am inside,
the more peace I have to share with others.
World peace really does begin with me.

315

I follow my inner star.
I am a shining example of love and light.

316

I take the things I think are "wrong" about me
and turn them into positive affirmations.

317

I inhale the precious breath of life;
and I allow my body, mind,
and emotions to relax.

318

I handle my own life with joy and ease.

319

I am proud that I can easily adapt to the ebb and flow of my life.

320

I am gentle, kind,
and patient with myself.
Those around me
reflect this
tender care.

321

I give love to all the animals who come into my life.
They are gifts from the Universe.

322

My body is always working toward optimal health.
I am happy and healthy.

323

Today is the future
I created yesterday.

324

I rejoice in the knowledge that I
have the power of my own mind
to use in any way I choose.

325

Everything in my life works now
and forevermore.

326

My thinking is peaceful,
calm, and centered.

327

I am thankful for all the days of my life
that I have lived so far. I am also thankful
for all the days I have yet to live.
Life is so good.

328

My good comes
from everywhere
and everyone and
everything.

329

The gateways
to wisdom and
knowledge
are
always
open
to me.

330

I constantly
have new insights.
My future is
glorious.

331

Whenever I travel, I am protected and safe.
I always have an enjoyable time.

332

I take time today to
bask in the love and light
of my life. What a
glorious day!

333

Forgiving makes me
feel free and light.
I forgive everyone,
including myself.

334

I am guided throughout this day to
make all the right choices. I only desire
that which is for my highest good.

335

I find joy and appreciation in
everything I say and do.

336

The joy in my life is
overflowing.
My life gets better
all the time.

337

I am open and receptive to all the good and
abundance in the Universe.

338

I create my own experiences. As I love and approve of myself and others, my life gets better and better.

339

All of my friends understand my needs.
I have many friends who love me.

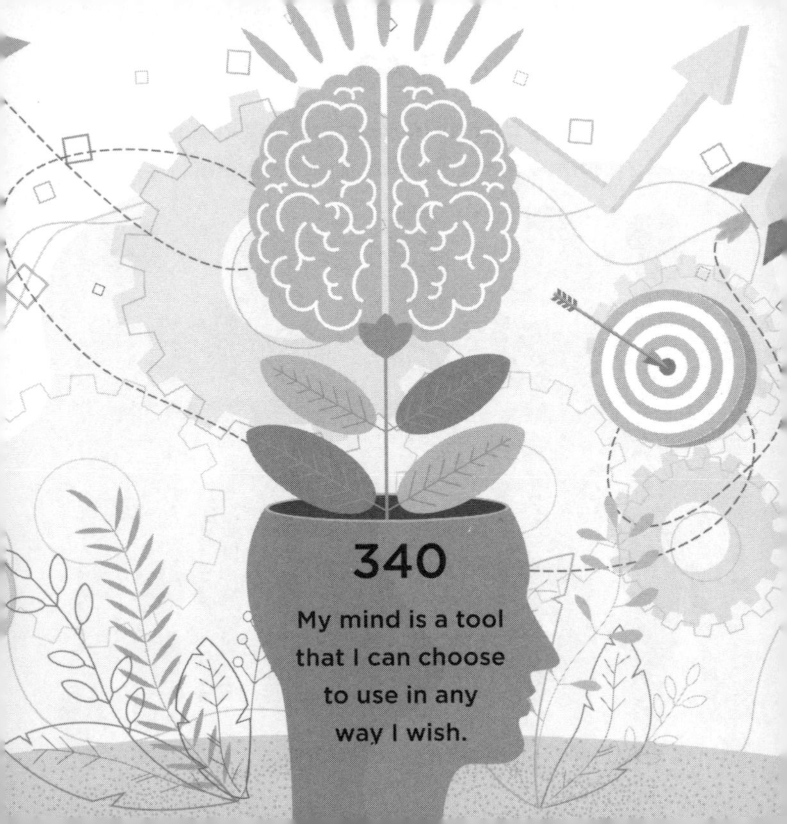

340

My mind is a tool
that I can choose
to use in any
way I wish.

341

I make time to do the things that I enjoy.
I get out and experience life in a new way.

342

All my needs and desires are met before I even ask.
All is well in my world.

343

Joyous new ideas
are circulating freely
within me.

344

I know that before
others will love me,
I have to love myself.
My self-love begins now.

345

I respect all the members of my family,
and they, in turn, respect me.

346

I view all experiences as opportunities
for me to learn and grow.

347

I see myself as beautiful, lovable, and appreciated.
I am proud to be me.

348

I deserve to enjoy life. I ask for what I want,
and I accept it with joy and pleasure.

349

My home fulfills all my needs and desires.
I fill my home with love.

350

I now free myself from destructive fears and doubts.

351

People love to be with me,
and I love to be with people.

352

It is my birthright to share
in the abundance and
prosperity of this world.

353

I only speak positively about those in my world.
Negativity has no part in my life.

354

Difficulties no longer burden me.
I easily solve all problems.

I am an open channel for creative ideas.

356

I am capable and organized. My efficiency is more than ample to get any job done.

357

I am empowered and confident.
I hold my head up high.

358

A smiling face and joyful, loving words are the best presents I can share with everyone I know.

359

I lovingly and joyously
accept my sexuality and
its expression.

360

I treat my partner with love and respect,
and receive the same in return.

361

I am willing to release all patterns of criticism.

362

I am a decisive and productive person. I follow through with tasks that I start and make no excuses.

363

I read books that enrich my soul
and give me food for thought.
There is always more to learn.

364

The love from my heart flows
joyously through my body.

365

I express love and gratitude for all I have learned and all I have accomplished. I look forward with joyous anticipation to each new day of my life. All is well in my world!

ALSO BY LOUISE HAY

Books

The Adventures of Lulu (children's book with Dan Olmos)
All Is Well (with Mona Lisa Schulz, M.D., Ph.D.)
The Bone Broth Secret (with Heather Dane)
Colors & Numbers
The Essential Louise Hay Collection
Everyday Positive Thinking
Experience Your Good Now!
Gratitude: A Way of Life (also available in Spanish)
Heal Your Body (also available in Spanish)
Heal Your Body A–Z
Heal Your Mind (with Mona Lisa Schulz, M.D., Ph.D.)
Heart Thoughts
I Can Do It® (book-with-download)
Inner Wisdom
I Think, I Am! (children's book with Kristina Tracy)
Letters to Louise (also available in Spanish)

Life Loves You (with Robert Holden)

Life! Reflections on Your Journey

Love Your Body

Love Yourself, Heal Your Life Workbook

Loving Yourself to Great Health (with Ahlea Khadro and Heather Dane)

Meditations to Heal Your Life (also available in Spanish)

Mirror Work

Modern-Day Miracles (Louise & Friends)

101 Ways to Happiness

Painting The Future: A Tales of Everyday Magic Novel (with Lynn Lauber)

The Power Is Within You (also available in Spanish)

The Present Moment

The Times of Our Lives (Louise & Friends)

Trust Life

21 Days to Master Affirmations

You Can Create an Exceptional Life (with Cheryl Richardson, also available in Spanish)

You Can Heal Your Heart (with David Kessler)

You Can Heal Your Life (also available in a gift edition
   and in Spanish)
You Can Heal Your Life Companion Book

Audio Programmes

All Is Well (audiobook)
Anger Releasing
Cancer
Change and Transition
Dissolving Barriers
Embracing Change
Evening Meditation
Feeling Fine Affirmations
Forgiveness/Loving the Inner Child
Heal Your Mind (audiobook)
How to Love Yourself (audiobook)
I Can Do It® (audiobook)
Life Loves You (audiobook)
Love Your Body (audiobook)
Meditations for Loving Yourself to Great Health

Meditations for Personal Healing
Morning and Evening Meditations
101 Power Thoughts
Overcoming Fears (audiobook)
The Power Is Within You (audiobook)
The Power of Your Spoken Word
Receiving Prosperity
Self-Esteem Affirmations (subliminal)
Self-Healing
Stress-Free (subliminal)
Subliminal Affirmations for Positive Self-Esteem
Totality of Possibilities
What I Believe and Deep Relaxation
You Can Heal Your Heart (audiobook)
You Can Heal Your Life (audiobook, also available in Spanish)
You Can Heal Your Life Study Course

Videos

Dissolving Barriers
Doors Opening
Painting the Future: Tales of Everyday Magic
Receiving Prosperity
You Can Heal Your Life, The Movie (available in standard and expanded editions)
You Can Trust Your Life (with Cheryl Richardson)

Inspirational Cards

Heart Thoughts Cards (mobile app)
How to Love Yourself Cards (mobile app and deck)
I Can Do It® Cards (mobile app)
Life Loves You Cards (mobile app and deck with Robert Holden)
Power Thought Cards (mobile app and deck)

Journals

The Gift of Gratitude: A Guided Journal for Counting Your Blessings

How to Love Yourself: A Guided Journal for Discovering Your Inner Strength and Beauty

Calendar

I Can Do It®️ Calendar (for each individual year)

Online Courses

Loving Yourself: 21 Days to Improved Self-Esteem with Mirror Work (with Robert Holden)

You Can Trust Your Life: Create Your Best Year Yet (with Cheryl Richardson)

ABOUT THE AUTHOR

LOUISE HAY was an inspirational teacher who educated millions since the 1984 publication of her bestseller *You Can Heal Your Life*, which has more than 50 million copies in print worldwide. Renowned for demonstrating the power of affirmations to bring about positive change, Louise was the author of more than 30 books for adults and children, including the bestsellers *The Power Is Within You* and *Heal Your Body*. In addition to her books, Louise produced numerous audio and video programs, card decks, online courses, and other resources for leading a healthy, joyous, and fulfilling life.

Websites:
www.louisehay.com, www.healyourlife.com, and
www.facebook.com/louiselhay

Hay House Titles of Related Interest

YOU CAN HEAL YOUR LIFE, the movie,
starring Louise Hay & Friends
(available as an online streaming video)
www.hayhouse.com/louise-movie

THE SHIFT, the movie,
starring Dr. Wayne W. Dyer
(available as an online streaming video)
www.hayhouse.com/the-shift-movie

***

All of the above are available at www.hayhouse.co.uk

***

CONNECT WITH
HAY HOUSE
ONLINE

🌐 hayhouse.co.uk   **f** @hayhouse

📷 @hayhouseuk   🐦 @hayhouseuk

▶ @hayhouseuk   ♪ @hayhouseuk

*Find out all about our latest books & card decks • Be the first
to know about exclusive discounts • Interact with our authors
in live broadcasts • Celebrate the cycle of the seasons with us
• Watch free videos from your favourite authors •
Connect with like-minded souls*

'*The gateways to wisdom and knowledge
are always open.*'

Louise Hay